MORNING

Last Poems

Don Welch

CONTENTS

FOR THE RHYME OF IT. . . .

AND THE REST OF IT...

For the thistle, the nettle, the burdock, the belladonna,
And a small wind above them, a sleepy cloud, silence.

--Czeslaw Milosz

FOR THE RHYME OF IT. . . .

ON THE WAY TO SCHOOL

Morning has no reason
to ride the bus again

after bullies beat it up
and split its chin.

But here is Morning
with its backpack on

in seat One again,
Morning, on the street

to Hell, a kid
of bright withins.

FOR THE GIRL, AGE 12, WHO LIKES ROBERT FROST

Reed so young with big sky eyes
and knees like bell-bong clappers,
the quicksilver of your mouth's surprise
runs ore-veined through the matter

of pasture springs and snowy woods,
leaves of Robert's choosing.
You thank the poems with your assent
to bell-tongue Robert's musings.

So, go with the grace of his old finger,
swing your songs to earthward.
Dare the dancing of a singer
whose note's as rare as you are.

SONG

When I was young
and juiceful,
green of bone,
at ease,

I treated bricks
on sidewalks
as if they were
red keys,

ones I ran over
lightly,
toeing forth
melodies—

oh, the air I heard
so slightly
was a sheer
mortality.

FOR EMILY

When martins sit the wires like notes,
chords of birds to see,
the morning is a tourist
with purple melodies.

With such a song at sunrise,
with such majesty,
the air's so quick and feathered
it assumes intricacies.

So if song can set its wings and sail
between the wires and trees,
legato are some mornings
full of thoughts that tease.

WITH GOOD MUSIC IN MY HEAD

I've known the childlessness of mornings,
the illnesses of souls.
I've walked with cancered tough ones
and navigated poles.

With cracks on sidewalks as my maps,
past academics, pinched;
when the sun's been cruel to shingles
and inch-worms out of inch.

I've walked through slogs of grayness
with good music in my head.
Bird-witted, run-footed,
I've been congenitally well-bred.

YOUNG

Young, we were fin-fliers, silver flairs.
"Come," you said, before
encrustations could turn us doctrinaire,
before we would gill despairs.

And I did. Following you,
I slipped nets, leaped dams and weirs.
What I brooked, my love,
was no more tangled than your hair.

Now old, we snorkel memories,
prolonging swimming in their light.
You, the one I've loved and confided in,
the long-haired star for my black nights.

ALMOST AN ODE

How can I, good sun,
choose a face for your bright eye;
an old man whose thoughts turn
to cold necessities?

Yet, here you are again,
a warmth in my stone tree,
one that floods my twisted limbs
full of cruelties.

The dog I walk has splayed legs
(good for any tree?).
The dog I walk has grateful eyes.
The hound I walk is me.

I GET UP FOR MORNING

I get up for morning.
I put my pants on for the sun.
I try to loop my mind around Athens.
I buckle up for love.

I have the urge for it;
it gathers like a breeze.
My ligaments, Nordic,
grow stretched out, full of ease.

Socrates is my companion,
old fencer, full of *whys*?,
carrying staples for the morning
and a pry-bar for my mind.

So, we walk together
(with DNA between?).
I like to be seen with Socrates.
He says he'll consider me.

PLAYING VOLLEYBALL WITH THE SUN

Ready, knees loose
for his serve,
ready for the whistle,
your soles dug in with love;

looking at a net strung
from pole to pole,
its tape, light orange,
your tights on, ready to roll—

you, in thumb-lock,
poised to forearm his ball,
to jump into a morning
whose end-line is your soul's--

so, here comes Helios, serving
his thermal ball.
Grand-daughters, in your youthful crouch,
set it for us all.

FOR THE KID STILL DELIVERING THE GOODS

Southern Kansas. Revival meetings. Bill Kloefkorn.
Whose voice, baptized in the words we call King James,
grew deep and long in lines so surely formed
they hang in air, ready for our out-stretched fingers.

What was it that let him feel in words both
a wit and wisdom, then let him finger them
into a music Orpheus once tuned?
To transfigure air into thrown song?

In a land where there's always a rock, a humbling
stone,
one which takes Spring from our cock-sure voices
and throws them back a season, he was the grown kid
on the bike delivering beacons to our homes.

How he still grand-daughters summers.
And leads us north-by-northwest, organ-toned.

FOR SHIRLEY B.

This morning, in this world of disposable lies,
excellence pools.

A light without carp, one without suckers,
it moments our poor afternoons.

And you, still remembered by words,
how dark your boat, how narrow the fit

of its doom. But your verse?
Full of sense and strong waves how it moves.

So like this morning which kept to itself
until it inhabited our rooms.

ARTHUR PIERCE, SCRIBE

From the long shelf of the past,
and through his warming window,
coarse-robed voices came to him
as he sat sandaled--

In the reign of No-Tongue's son,
Wordstun was appointed scribe,
a monk whose inhabited initials
shunned the Viscerals' lives.

When Law was destroyed, and no plunder
seized there, Wordstun died.
He was hallowed to heaven
at Worthchurch, where he lies--

and in that light he picked up
pens to fit his eyes,
dipping them, and his left hand,
into morning's careful skies.

YOU ASK ABOUT WORDS

I'd like to think they're like good mornings,
ones which go out one after another, in hill hurries,
with nights as their fasts.

And you, who've been creatured for words,
which make your days better?
Go greening, with noses, which credit letters?

*

Because right now there are mouth men filling up the
air,
peacocks settling for their tails,
and surrealists hugging themselves to death.

On your road to The Wise Stutter,
tag and number only
the best gifts of your breaths.

SO, WHAT IS IT TO SPECIFY MORNING?

That temperament of the sky,
with its orange pupil, high?

Squeezed of everything not fair,
what inclines it to risks in air?

To pit itself against cynics,
those with cruel laughs?

But what goes deliberate, over fundaments,
a disposition for our lives,

if not morning in an age of words
that has turned our songs to cries?

HOW TO GET INTO SHAPE FOR A GOOD MORNING

First, it is important to lie very still,
to be as attentive as a bead on raw silk.

To have a warm cave for a mouth,
and, for a few minutes at least,

a negative belly. In the afternoon
you can tune in to the channels of sadness.

You can lie down in the moss of yourself
and think of God as a petrified tree.

But now, outside, clear pearls are
necklacing the willows.

They are of great price for the breeze.

THE IRIS

This morning the iris,
fertile, deeply purple,
is presenting itself to hard woods.

But what can our oaks say
to this mystery of physics,
this propulsion of color,

this *esse* without words?
Now a bee drops by,
the transitive of a rooted lover.

It enters this oboe of morning.
It kisses its alto of color.

WHEN WE ASK YOU IN

When we ask you in,
unequaled light,
you're so egalitarian
in our rooms less bright

you kiss our music stands
with clefs of light,
your signature
on our arthritic nights.

And when we ask you in,
sweet broom of the air,
you sweep our rooms
with angels' hair,

our pains running backward,
counter to the sun;
you, our young-ward,
liquid one.

ON AN OVERCAST MORNING

--after G. M. Hopkins

Morning, are you grieving
over the dark still leafing?

When you are orange,
do you question why?

Rising over reasons
where reasons clotted lie?

No matter then your age,
you are morning just the same.

You, old time expressed,
but each day new, birth-blessed.

You are the light we were born for.
It is not orange we mourn for.

SILENCE

You, with the longest tongue,
what have you told me on my morning walks?

That there are moments when you fall upon the roses
and their petals embrace?

Times when as the thinnest lip of distance
you almost speak?

You, the gravity in my blood,
the white choir in my mind,

what you've been for years is love
and the gleaming dorsal fin of time.

MORNING, IN A LONG-TERM-CARE HOME

Out there, the hackberry is the grayest tree.
It has no variety in its leafless limbs.
It is a monotone for every sky and wind.
Among the spruce, a gnarled between.

From here we can see toadstools between its toes,
fleshy tables serving up malaise.
Above, where the bark's been eaten away,
nothing stares from empty holes.

Yet who says the hackberry's day-blind like the stars?
Or can't feel the run-a-limb of water?
Isn't there something in it, gaunt, in showers,
that remembers the leaf-laughter of its daughters?
Out there, beyond the sun-room of this home,
the tree that's standing by our father?

OVER

When all of this is over,
and you have buried death again,

I want you to let the light
take time to be the light again.

I want you to walk so softly
no one can track your steps, no guess.

I want you to let the wind
relieve your faces with its clear mask.

AND THE REST OF IT. . . .

THE WHITE BLACKBIRD

There it was, a wonder perched in time,
a pearl-eyed thing feathering off into long wings.

What it sang was the last note indexed in the book
of silence. What it sorted was every sight

not related to salvation. And there, among
the split wood in my backyard, I let that bird

show me what to shed, silent as I stood there,
my axe in its white wind.

ARCHANGELS

As the cold fell at a brutal slant,
riveting the iridescence into your pigeons' necks,
I stood there, learning that certain moments
are gifts to certain heads.

And when your Archangels flew to roosts,
wrapping me in holy time,
I remember you yelling, "Kid, go home!
I can see your damn knees knocking in the cold!"

Warloski, how many Archangels came down to you as
    suns,
birds of the highest order of colors,
with ignitions in their lusters--
how many for the dark days of the cold?

You, grizzled, crippled, looking from your window
at birds lit up by love?

AT AGE 11

When innocence was a good kid who hung around
longer,
and death lived two or three neighborhoods over
in the crushed side of a pickup;

when on Saturdays, Fourth Ward School was a wake of
desks,
and in our backyard
morning had an Adamic sun;

when clouds were only backdrops for my tumblers,
exotic pigeons full of somersaults,
and the sky held time without division;

when, except for the generations of my pigeons,
I was oblivious to what would come. . . .

MORNING, THEN AND NOW

I grew up chasing Muscovy ducks and guineas.
This was before Jewish numbers, German signatures,
    the burning of blood.

And later, as my bashful hand stuttered into yours,
on the other side of the world, barbed wire raked the
    eyes of girls,

boys were gassed and burned;
were turned to silence, into silence turned.

Now as I sit here watching a plane streak over,
hurrying toward more urban truths,

among its travelers are surely those
looking down on us through their windows.

I wonder, what they will say of this fly-over place
when I'm gone,

when overhead more airships are trailing
the hair of old women?

Sure in their seats, with more privilege,
will they be better borne,

hurtling, as this metal paragraph is hurtling above me,
straight toward the hag-eye of the moon?

AFTER THE SUICIDE BOMBING

Gluts
of flesh
in the trees

and entrails
of black
blood,

where
breaths
had been

clearer
than
morning

and
had flown
like invisible

birds.

THIS MORNING

I found a feather in the alley,
so light it had not in its fall
disturbed the dust--

like you,
just dead--

the down parts
of your voice still soft with bloom
and unfretted by the winds.

THE MORNING'S PRAYER

Let me put my hand
on your young leg.
In the dry rut of my age
let me feel again
the music in its tendons;
pay homage to the nerves
that net your game.

Let me shoulder grace,
your lifts,
the way you walk on air.
Oil every crust
of my scabbed movements.
Take me above the rims
of my cares.

THE VERY OLD

The very old gather in parlors
like paddlefish dwindling
below dams.

They look out of small eyes
in spatulate heads.
They swim out dreams

that are boneless.
And as the wind drives
hard on the rocks,

stenciling frost
and sending grubs
deep into trees,

something in them
fattens the current,
takes no bait,

and avoids being snagged.
Something ancient,
resisting extinction.

Lugging, it lags.

SHUFFLING OUT TOWARD MORNING

After an hour in the infusion lab,
Taxol dripping into her,
fighting her cancer;

after sitting nauseous
next to a man
vomiting into a Pepsi cup,

she rose, palming the hall,
stooping only to pick up
a pen a doctor had dropped,

giving it back to the doctor
who had slipped it poorly
into his coat.

JOY

It was when, she said, her skin quivered
from the inside out, turning her shadow from dark
to light, like a morning flooding, overflowing.

From her bones came something
like the marrow of the sun,
a flush she gave to space.

Just as a blackbird on a shriveled stalk
can fill its shoulders with bright crying,
a reddening for everything that falls,

she said she could walk among the hateful
as if morning were within her,
her skin a miracle.

ABSENT

We met when you were
brushing drum-strokes,
when luck was "in" in a world
made fickle by its rolls.

And you, pick-up sticks
in your deft hands,
drummed into circumstance
a fortune which has stood

around us for our lives,
with a persistence
that's been feathered.
This morning,

in the language shadow,
I kissed you with my eyes.

*

Now, 10 a.m., you're gone.
The silence of this house
is your plain perfume,
as honest as the air in flower.

The kitchen clock tries
to true a room you care for
with hurt hands. The TV, black,
can only anti-matter strife.

But here where your reasons
have reason to remember,
your presence blooms. Absent,
you haunt this place with life.

AFTER ALL THESE YEARS

We have become a good silence,
we talk to each other
like light and its beams.

Years into love, we have reduced
our addictions to words,
to those black and white fixtures

of pleasures, of pains. Silent,
we look to what's wise,
good acts for our misshapen fingers.

And we hold on, we hold on
like a drop of good rain,
among cruelties, inanities, gutters.

OLD,

I appreciate the ghosts walking beside me,
　　　　their white shadows in the grass.

And on the other side of the lilies no weeping
　　　　asking for forgiveness.

What is congenital joy if not a music turning
　　　　upon tables in our brain stems?

For years I studied the tragedies
　　　　of the great ones.

I taught the young, almost all of whom
　　　　jumped the classics with their glands.

This morning I walk, rectified by word-work.
　　　　Old, I'm grateful for its trims.

THE GYM

I went in, the light so harsh
my body had no shadow.
High-up were banners,
with triumphs glued to felts.

In the center of the floor
an antelope, modernized and lacquered,
with mopheads dribbling on it,
was headed south.

And as I stood there,
I thought of Socrates' young men;
of those oiled, rubbed down,
the living trophies of their fathers.

And of Socrates himself,
who in honoring
the One within him,
shaped his life with *whys*?

I stood there, among
those of groin and limb,
with their fathers in their eyes.

TALKING TO FRED

This morning is like the picture of your life.

A picture ain't a thing.

It's just a picture?

Yep.

Then this morning isn't worth much?

No, it ain't.

This thing like morning.

It ain't a life.

NOON

Hear the moon groan?

No, I said,

as over my arm
the morning continued to hover.

*

Are you ready
for death?
she said.

If I'm not,
how useless
are the great books
I've read.

GOOD FRIDAY MORNING

They see me mowing,
the sun blazing its truth
through our laurels,
its rays on our paradise lost.

Jehovah's witnesses they
come, their Bible in hand,
and for a moment
we have our porch steps

in common. In Genesis,
for how long was there a courtesy
to listen? Before we became
sinful, lethal, consoled?

Who sat there before
revelation, before reason,
heart-first to what
knocked on their doors?

PLEASE DON'T LAUGH, BUT THIS MORNING

I decided to re-visit my soul,
before sleep became the rest
of me, before it turned
into the longest of lines.

Years ago I left it
off the point of a sandbar,
a spit well riddled of stones;
where out of the ocean

it had come at me
riding the crest of a wave;
where it had made of the water
a sparkling point in the air.

This morning, looking out,
I saw my soul coming in.
Welling, clearly elated,
it kept waving right up to my door.

I opened and stood there.
It left me more than ajar.

MY SHADOW,

you started
me well,
quickening me
over the snow
in what was
no bag race.

Young, you flew
like Mercury
before he out-sped
his twin;
before, turning
his back

on the earth,
the god took eternity in.
Shadow,
I thank you
for not outrunning
this man.

This morning
the sun is out,
our way is
straight-forward,
we walk in
lean skins.

Old,
I have no
better image
of whom
I might have been.

SILENCE, AGAIN

For years I've tried to map silence,
its islands of presence, its bays of absence,
the airs of its ethers and clouds.

In church, it lay in the folds of my hands.
In the infields of love, it was the catch in my throat.
Only occasionally was it a volcano

which blew through the roof of my mouth.
In the book of silence, its last chapter,
I'm still trying to sift the rest of it out:

the finest meanings of *silens, silere,*
and the unspoken letter in *doubt.*

THE PERFECT

60 years in coming,

it was the negative I'd tried to print,

and yesterday I saw it in a clearing,

in its finest hairs, upon a ground of chalk;

a thing without a scar,

in a time without a tense.

I had no words, no words at all,

for red fox sense.

About the Author

Don Welch was the Reynolds Chair of Poetry at the University of Nebraska at Kearney, where he recently completed his 50th year teaching English and Philosophy. He is the winner of a number of national prizes in poetry, the most significant being the Neruda Prize. His book of selected poetry, containing almost all of his prize-winning poems, is *Inklings* (Sandhills Press).

His most recent books of verse are *Gutter Flowers* (Logan House), *When Memory Gives Dust a Face* (Lewis-Clark Press), *Travels* (Finishing Lines Press) *Deliberations* (Backwaters Press), *Gnomes* (Stephen F. Austin University Press), and *In Times of Considerable Wars* (All Along Press). For years he was a poet in the public schools for the Nebraska Arts Council. He also served as a participant and consultant to the PBS film *The Last of the One-Room Schools.*

Acknowledgments

Book design by Dwaine Spieker
Cover photo by Erin Lane

ISBN: 978-1-304-77172-8

pigeonpress
611 W. 27
Kearney, NE 68845

www.ingramcontent.com/pod-product-compliance
Ingram Content Group UK Ltd.
Pitfield, Milton Keynes, MK11 3LW, UK
UKHW020217250726
13967UKWH00001B/56

9 781304 771728